Siwon's Story of
Kings of England

Written & Illustrated by
Siwon Lee

Prologue

Hello, My name is Siwon Lee and I am 12 years old. I like studying history. When I turned 12, I published a book about the history of the USA. My friends enjoyed my books and they learned more about the history of the USA. This motivated me to write a new book: Siwon's Story of Kings of England.

I also like to research and study new informations about world history. The history of England gave me more attention than any other countries. The fact that England became the strongest country in the world was fascinating. Writing this book also helped me to learn more information about England's history. During the editing process, I was able to step forward my grammar skill and editing skill.

Especially, the story of Kings and dynasties of England in the Middle Ages fascinates young readers including me. After Rome retreated from Britain in the 5th century, many leaders who owned lands tried to unite the kingdoms into one country. After a hundred years, England's first ruling dynasty, the House of Wessex, perished. Then, the Duke of Normandy, William I, invaded England in 1066. This is famously known as the "Norman Conquest." The invasion changed many things.

In this book, I will talk about the major changes that happened in the history of England: The Norman Conquest of William I, the Magna Carta of King John, the Hundred Years' War from Edward III to Henry VI, and the Wars of the Roses. You will learn England's history from William I to Queen Mary I in the Middle Ages.

You will find the same names for the English kings, so many people will be confused: grandfather, Henry IV; father, Henry V; son, Henry VI. So, I drew the family trees and portraits of the kings for the readers to understand. I hope you enjoy the story of England's kings in the Middle Ages.

I am specially grateful to my parents who inspired me to write my second book.

August 31, 2023
Written & Illustrated by Siwon Lee

Contents

Chapter 4: The Kings during the Wars of the Roses

Henry IV   Henry V   Henry VI   Edward IV   Edward V

Richard III

Chapter 5: The Kings in the House of Tudor

Henry VII   Henry VIII   Edward VI   Lady Jane Grey   Mary I

Epilogue

Family Tree of England Monarchs

The Kings in the House of the Normandy

The Kings in the House of the Anjou

The Kings in the House of the Plantagenet

The Kings during the Wars of the Roses

The Kings in the House of Tudor

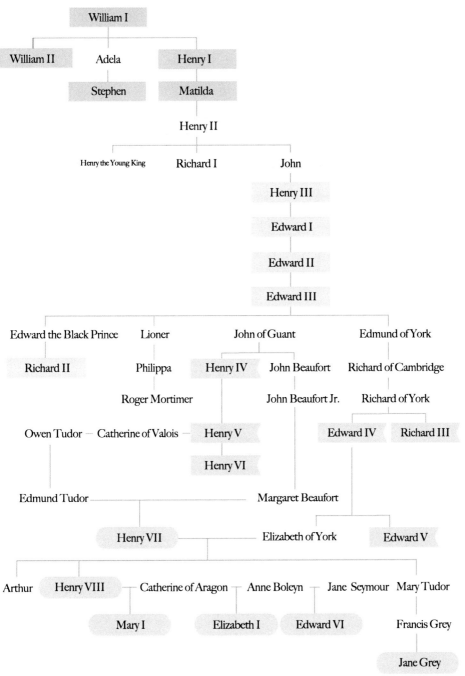

Chapter I:
The Kings
in the House of
the Normandy

Illustrated by Siwon Lee

This is the most famous picture of King William I. As you see, he is holding a fighting sword. Also, he is wearing gray armor.

William I

William I was born in 1028 in Normandy and was the illegitimate son of Robert II. He inherited the title of Duke of Normandy in 1035 at the age of seven. He was a descendant of the Viking hero Rollo (846-933). When he became an adult, he met the future English king, Edward the Confessor. He was a prince who had fled to Normandy because of the Danish invasion. Edward promised William that if he did not have a child, he would name William as his successor.

After Edward returned to England, he died childless on January 5, 1066. So, William thought that he would be the next king. Contrary to his expectation, the throne went to Harold II, who claimed that King Edward had appointed him as his successor. Understandably, William opposed this opinion and launched a civil war. As a result, William killed Harold. He also imprisoned Edgar II, who was selected as the last king of the Wessex dynasty. This is now known as the Norman Conquest.

William married Matilda of Flanders. She was the daughter of the Count of Flanders. As time passed, William was worried about the land that he needed to distribute to his children. William and Matilda had nine children, of which four were sons. His first son Robert had a very unpleasant relationship with his father. He even formed a rebellion against William and was sent to France. Before William died, Robert received Normandy from his father and became the next Duke of Normandy. William's second son, Richard, died early at the age of 15~16 because of a hunting accident.

William's third son, William Junior, was awarded the throne of England instead of his older brother, Robert. He became William II after the death of William I. Henry, the fourth son of William I, also became the King of England when his brother, William II, died childless at the age of 43.

William I died on September 9, 1087. His greatest achievement was conquering England and establishing a new dynasty, the House of Normandy. Because of this achievement, he is known as William the Conqueror. He was the Duke of Normandy from 1066 to 1087. Then, he was the King of England from 1060 to 1087. One of his daughters, Princess Adela, married Stephen, the Count of Blois. She then became the Countess of Blois. One of her sons, Stephan of Blois (1092~1154), later became the King of England in 1135.

Illustrated by Siwon Lee

This is the most famous picture of King William II. He is sitting in front of the palace door with many accessories.

William II

William II was born between 1056 and 1060. He was the third son of King William I and his wife, Matilda of Flanders. He inherited England on September 26, 1087. During his reign, he became increasingly unpopular among his people because he taxed them heavily. Surprisingly, he was a bachelor and never married.

He fought against his brother Henry for lands that he wanted to have. After a decade, they made peace. While William was hunting with Henry, he was shot by an arrow. The person who shot the arrow remained unknown. This is one of the most famous mysteries in England.

William II died on August 2, 1100, between the age of 39 and 44. He reigned as the king of England from 1087 to 1100.

This is a picture of King Henry I. He has a miniature castle. Also, he is sitting in front of the castle's door like his brother, King William II.

Henry I

Henry I was born in 1068 in England. He was the last child of William I and Matilda of Flanders. He became the King of England in 1100 after his brother William II died childless. Henry married Matilda of Scotland in 1110. They had four children, but only two survived: his daughter Matilda and son William. Unfortunately, his only surviving legitimate son, Prince William, died at the age of 17 on account of a ship accident. The only surviving child was his daughter, Matilda.

However, the death of the prince created a big problem. England never had a ruling queen or female rulers before. Since England's first dynasty, the House of Wessex was made up only of male rulers. As Henry did not have any legitimate sons, who could succeed him, he consequently decided that Matilda would be his heir. The nobility was opposed to this decision.

Henry I died on December 1, 1135, between the age of 66 and 67. He was the King of England from 1100 to 1135 and Duke of Normandy from 1106 to 1135. Some interesting facts about Henry I are that he had more than 20 children, and his wife was a descendant of Alfred the Great who had saved England from Viking's invasion.

23

Illustrated by Siwon Lee

This is the picture of King Stephen. Like his two uncles, King William and King Henry, he is sitting in front of the palace door. He also has a miniature castle and is wearing a crown.

Stephen

Stephen was born in 1092 or 1096 in France. He was the third son of Adela of Normandy (the daughter of King William I) and Atian, the Duke of Blois. Henry I had decided to make his legitimate daughter, Matilda, the Queen after his only legitimate son, William died. As aforementioned, England had only male rulers since 519.

From this point on, Stephen decided to become the successor to the throne. In 1035, King Henry I died. Matilda went abroad because of her marriage to Jeffery V, the Count of Anjou. Stephen came to England and declared himself King. Matilda believed that he had illegally obtained the throne from her. Therefore, the conflict led to a civil war, won by Matilda in 1141.

Unfortunately, Matilda was not recognized as the true ruler in England because she was an Empress in Germany. So, Stephen's side dethroned her and gave the throne back to Stephen. The civil war continued, and Matilda's son Henry fought against Stephen. When Stephen's son Eustace died suddenly, Stephen made Henry his successor. Stephen died on October 25, 1154, between the age of 57 and 62.

Stephan was the King of England from 1035 to 1041 in his first term and from 1041 to 1054 in his second term. He was the Duke of Normandy from 1044 to 1054.

Illustrated by Siwon Lee

Here is the picture of Matilda. She is wearing a red cape and a crown, like her grandfather William I, uncle William II, father Henry I, and cousin Stephen.

Matilda

Matilda was born on February 7, 1102. She was the first daughter of King Henry I and Matilda of Scotland. Matilda married the Holy Roman Emperor Henry V at the age of 12. During the marriage, Matilda's younger brother William died, and Matilda was to be her father's successor. When Matilda was 23 years old, her husband Henry died at the age of 38. As Matilda and the emperor had no children, she had no reason to stay in the empire. As a result, she came back to England.

In 1028, Matilda decided to marry Jeffery V, the Count of Anjou. When she was in France, her father, King Henry, died and her cousin Stephen declared himself King. However,

Matilda dethroned Stephen in 1041 and declared herself the English Queen. However, she was not authorized to rule in the royal system in England because she was well-adjusted in Germany. So, the English dethroned her, and Stephen took back the throne. Because of this, she is not usually considered a queen of England. Fortunately, her son Henry fought for her and won the war. As Stephen's son Eustace died suddenly, Henry became Stephen's successor.

As a result, Matilda became the Queen, Mother of the new dynasty that would continue for hundreds of years, the House of Anjou. Matilda died on September 10, 1167, at the age of 65. She was an empress of the Holy Roman Empire from 1114 to 1125. Then, she declared herself the queen of England from 1141 to 1148.

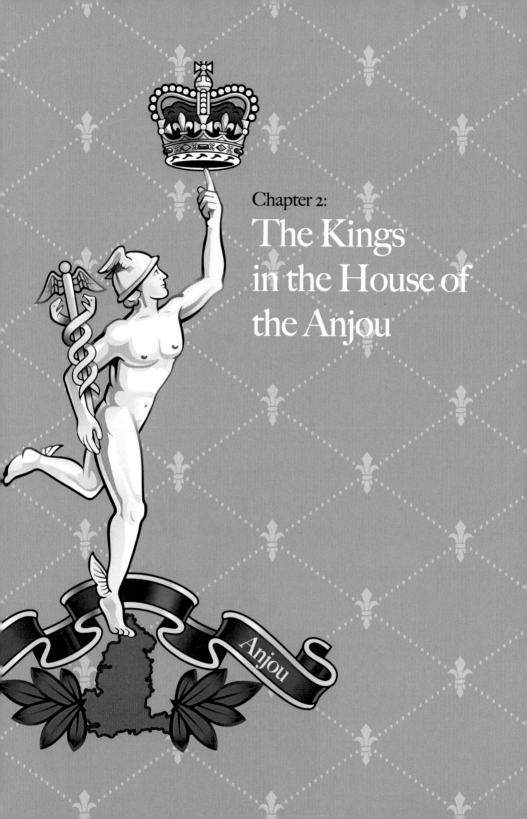

Chapter 2:
The Kings
in the House of
the Anjou

Illustrated by Siwon Lee

This is one of the most famous pictures of King Henry II. He is sitting on the with a cushion. Also, he is wearing a gold crown on his head.

Henry II

Henry Ⅱ was born on March 5, 1133, in France. He was the first son of Matilda and her second husband, Jeffery V, the Count of Anjou. He established the Anjou dynasty, which would continue for 331 years. When King Stephen died, Henry became the next king of England. Before his reign, Henry was married to Eleanor of Aquitaine in 1152. Eleanor was 30 years old, whereas Henry was 19. Eleanor had first been married to King Louis Ⅶ of France because her father, William 10th, the Duke of Aquitaine, wanted to secure her under French protection.

Henry Ⅱ was crowned with Eleanor. At first, they were happy

together. Henry received many French lands because of his marriage to Eleanor. In addition to Aquitaine, Henry got Maine, Touraine, Gascony, Poitiers, and Anjou. Those lands were constituted into one big empire: the Anjou Empire (1154-1214).

Henry and Eleanor had eight children: William, Matilda, Henry the Young King, Richard I, Jeffery II, Eleanor, Joan, and King John. Five of their children were sons, but their first son, William, died early. The second son, Young Henry, was a famous skilled fighter. So, Henry made him co-king of England, co-duke of Normandy, and co-count of Anjou. Young Henry married Margaret of France, who was the third daughter of King Louis VIII. Interestingly, Louis VIII of France was the first husband of Henry's mother, Eleanor.

There was a big problem, and Young Henry decided to dethrone his father, Henry II, with his brothers: Richard, Jeffery, and John. His mother, Queen Eleanor, also agreed with their decision and supported her sons. However, their force of arms was defeated, and Young Henry died in 1183 at the age of 28. To make matters worse, Eleanor was imprisoned for 16 years.

After she was released, she supported her sons again.

Therefore, Richard, Jeffery, and John attacked their father, Henry II and dethroned him. During the invasion, three of Henry's daughters were married: Matilda to Henry, the Lion of Bavaria and Saxony; Eleanor to King Alfonso VIII of Castile; Joan to William II of Sicily. In 1189, King Henry was heartbroken over the betrayal of his family. He died at the age of 56, and the throne went to his third son, Richard I .

Henry II was the Duke of Normandy and Count of Anjou, Maine, Touraine from 1151 to 1189. He was also the Count of Aquitaine, Gascony, and Poitiers from 1152 to 1189. Finally, he was the King of England from 1154 to 1189. He conquered Wales and united Ireland. His great achievement was establishing the Anjou Empire by uniting French lands to England.

Illustrated by Siwon Lee

Here is the picture of Henry the Young King. He is sitting on a king's chair in a palace. He is wearing a crown and a gown like the former kings and queens of England.

Henry the Young King

Henry, the Young King, was born in England on February 28, 1155. He was the second son of King Henry II and his wife, Eleanor of Aquitaine. When his brother William died at the age of two, he became his father's successor. As he fought like a warrior, King Henry II made his son the co-king of England. Young Henry married Margaret of France, who was the daughter of Louis VII of France. Louis was the first husband of Eleanor, who divorced in 1152.

Young Henry made a plan to attack his father by forming a rebellion with his brothers, and this plan was supported by their mother, Eleanor. However, his father's army was superior to the one he had borrowed from his father-in-law, King Louis VII. He then tried to sign a peace treaty with his father. However, before the treaty progressed, he died of dysentery in 1183 at the age of 28. He had one son, William, who sadly died soon after birth.

Young Henry was the co-king of England, co-duke of Normandy, and co-count of Anjou and Maine from 1170 to 1183. The most interesting fact about him is that he was married to Margaret of France when he was just five years old and Margaret was two. Like most marriages in the middle ages, this was a political marriage. Henry II and Louis VII had resolved their fight through this political marriage.

Here is the most famous picture of Richard I. Like a lion king, he is holding a fighting sword and shield. Also, he is wearing a silver and gold crown.

Richard I

Richard I was born in England on September 8, 1157. He was the third son of King Henry II and Eleanor of Aquitaine. As the third son, he was not expected to inherit the English throne. However, when his oldest brother William died at the age of three, his elder brother Henry was an heir to the throne in 1170 at the age of 15.

Henry fought against his father by forming a rebellion with his brothers: Richard, Jeffery, and John. Like his brother Henry, Richard borrowed his army from the French King Phillip II. His brother Jeffery died before the plan succeeded. The rebellion finally succeeded in 1189. Then, Richard became the King of

England, and John was made the Duke of Aquitaine. Their mother, Eleanor, became the queen dowager.

Richard went on the Third Crusade, which progressed from 1189 to 1192. He is known as Richard the Lion heart. When he was walking around a battlefield without any armor, an arrow hit him, and he died nine months later in England. He died in his mother's arms. He was the King of England for nine years, but he stayed there for only six months before he died at the age of 41. Though he had no legitimate children with his queen, Berengaria of Navarre, he had an illegitimate son, Philip of Cognac. However, the throne went to his youngest brother John.

Richard was the co-duke of Aquitaine from 1172 to 1199. Then, he was the Count of Maine from 1186 to 1199. Finally, he was the Duke of Normandy, the Count of Anjou, and the King of England from 1189 to 1199. All of his titles were inherited by his brother John, except the title Duke of Anjou. That title went to his nephew, Arthur, who was the son of his younger brother Jeffery.

There is one sentence that talks about Richard. "I was a bad son, a bad husband, a bad king, but a brave and lightened soldier."

He is famous for being a great and spectacular warrior king. In contrast, his brother John was notorious as an evil king. The most interesting fact about King Richard is that his mother, Eleanor, was the true ruler of England when she reigned as the regent for many years. Eleanor even rescued her son when he was captured by the Holy Roman Emperor Henry VI.

This is the picture of King John. He is wearing both white and red robes. Also, he is wearing a red and gold crown which has many gems with diverse colors.

John

King John was born on December 24, 1166. He was the last child and son of King Henry II and Eleanor of Aquitaine. John had three older brothers and three older sisters who were all kings and queens. His elder brothers, Henry and Richard, were kings of England. However, as they died childless, the throne went to their next living brother John.

Yet, their diseased middle brother, Jeffery, had a 13-year-old son, Arthur, whom the French believed to be the rightful king. While John was occupying the throne, his mother, Eleanor, supported him. Arthur attacked his grandmother, but John saved Eleanor and killed his nephew, Arthur. Then, he claimed the title, the Count of Anjou, from his nephew.

As John wanted to sign a peace treaty with France, he sent Eleanor to Spain. Eleanor met her two granddaughters and judged that the younger, Blanche, was suitable for marriage. So, young Blanche married Louis, the Dauphin of France. However, this happened before John killed his nephew Arthur.

Furthermore, John created some trouble. His second wife, Isabella, the Countess of Angouleme, had planned to marry one of the French nobles. However, John illegally married her using the English king's right. Therefore, the French King Phillip called John to his palace.

John disobeyed the French king's order. As a French noble, he had to obey the French king's order. Because of his disobedience, Phillip II had reasons to attack and invade the French lands that belonged to John. The French occupied Normandy, Maine, and Poitiers except for some lands, and the Anjou Empire broke up. From that point on, it was called the Plantagenet Empire until 1242.

John wanted to reform the empire, so he taxed the nobles heavily and gathered their army to attack France. As the nobles expected, the forces were defeated, and John lost again. The nobles were disappointed on account of this tragedy. They formed a rebellion and forced John to sign a document called the Magna Carta. This document limited the king's power. For example, before the Magna Carta, the king could do anything he wanted, even if the nobles did not agree. However, by virtue of the Magna Carta, the king could not tax the people or nobles without the nobles' agreement. This was signed in 1215, one year before John died. In 1216, John died at the age of 49.

The throne went to Louis, the Dauphin of France, because of his invasion. However, one year later, he was kicked out of England. Due to this case, he is not usually counted among the kings of England. The throne then went to King John's 10-year-old son, Prince Henry, and John's second wife became Henry's regent. The nobles were also included in the regency council.

John was first married to Isabella, the Countess of Gloucester, but they divorced in 1199. Then, John married another Isabella, the Countess of Angouleme. They had five children: Henry, Richard, Joan, Isabella, and Eleanor.

John first reigned as the Lord of Ireland from 1177 to 1216. Then, he was the Duke of Normandy, Count of Maine, and

Count of Poitiers from 1199 to 1204. Finally, he was the King of England and Duke of Aquitaine from 1199 to 1216. Also, he reigned as the Count of Angouleme with his wife, Isabella of Angouleme. There is a phrase: "King John represents the worst king, but Queen Elizabeth II represents the best monarch."

Some interesting facts about John were that his first daughter, Joan, was married to Alexander II of Scotland. Then, she became Queen of Scotland. His second daughter, Isabella, was married to Frederick II, Holy Roman Emperor, and she became the Holy Roman Empress. His last daughter, Eleanor, was married twice: first, to William Marshal, the second to Earl of Pembroke. When he died, she married Simon de Montfort, the 6th Earl of Leicester, who attacked and imprisoned King Henry III and Edward I.

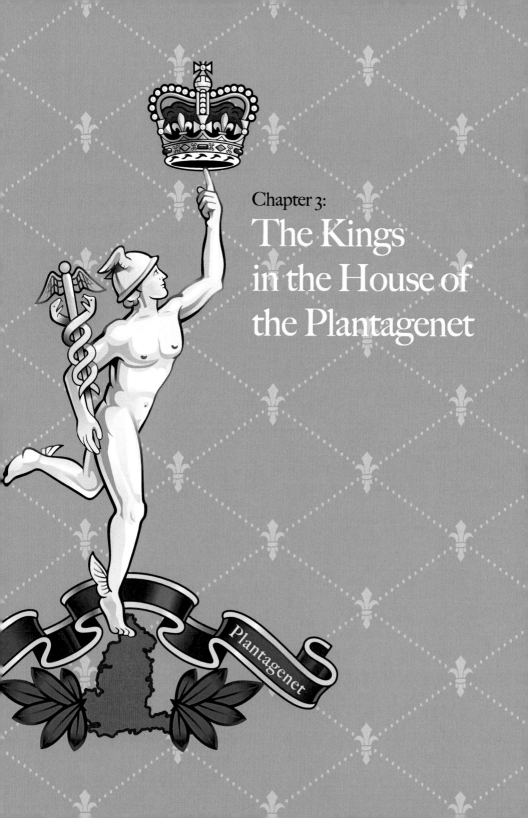

Chapter 3:
The Kings in the House of the Plantagenet

Illustrated by Siwon Lee

This is the most famous picture of King Henry Ⅲ. As you see, he is lying down with his crown. Unlike other kings, he is not sitting, but he is wearing the crown.

Henry III

Henry Ⅲ was born on October 1, 1207. He was the first son of King John and his second wife, Isabella. In 1216, his father, King John, died of dysentery. As a result, Henry ascended the throne as the King of England at the age of nine.

There were two regents from 1216 to 1227. First was William Marshal, the first Earl of Pembroke, who reigned as regent from 1216 to 1219. Then, Hubert de Burgh reigned as Henry Ⅲ's second regent from 1219 to 1227. When King Henry reached the age of 20, he dreamed of taking revenge on the nobles, as he believed that his father had died because of them.

One day, he got a letter from the Pope, who made the promise:

"If you give me money during the war between Sicily and the Pope, I will make your second son Edmund the king of Sicily." Henry wanted to collect the money by taxing the nobles. However, the nobles opposed him and stopped paying taxes to King Henry. Fortunately, he could send the supporting money to the Pope.

Henry III started to ignore the Magna Carta, and the nobles were furious at his actions. So, Simon de Montfort, the brother-in-law of Henry III, formed a rebellion and imprisoned King Henry and Prince Edward. However, Prince Edward defeated him and crowned his father the King of England once again. Even though King Henry was still King, Prince Edward was really in charge.

Henry III died on November 16, 1272, at the age of 65. He was the King of England, Duke of Aquitaine, and Lord of Ireland from 1216 to 1272. He married Eleanor of Provence in 1236 at the age of 28. They had five children: Edward, Margaret, Beatrice, Edmund, and Catherine. Finally, he saw the destruction of the Plantagenet Empire, which had been renamed from the Anjou Empire.

Illustrated by Siwon Lee

This is one of the famous pictures of King Edward I . Like most medieval kings, he is wearing a red cape and a gold crown with many gems.

Edward I

Edward I was born on June 17 or 18, 1239. He was the first son of King Henry III and his wife Eleanor of Provence. When he was 16, Edward married Eleanor of Castile, the daughter of King Ferdinand III of Castile and his second wife Joan, the Countess of Ponthieu. She was also the great granddaughter of Eleanor of England.

When Edward was 26, he was imprisoned along with his father by his uncle, Simon de Montfort. However, he escaped and won the war against Simon de Montfort. In 1272, he became the King of England at the age of 33. He is known as Edward Long shanks because of his height. He is also known as the Hammer of Scots since his reign achieved the subjection of Scotland.

When Edward became king, he first conquered Wales. Then, he launched military attacks on Scotland. Fortunately, he could occupy Scotland, but there was a riot by William Wallace and Robert the Bruce. However, they were defeated, and Wallace was killed. In addition, Robert was sent to Ireland. In 1307, King Edward died at the age of 68. The cause of his death was later stated as dysentery while he was fighting with Scotland. The throne passed to his oldest surviving son, Edward, who was 23 years old.

Edward I had 19 children from his two marriages to Eleanor of Castile and Margaret of France. The children were: Catherine; Joanna; John; Henry; Eleanor; Juliann; Joan of Acre; Alphonso, Earl of Chester; Margaret; Berengaria; an unknown daughter; Mary of Woodstock; an unknown son; Elizabeth of Rhuddlan; Edward II; Thomas, the first Earl of Norfolk; Edmund of Woodstock, the first Earl of Kent; and finally Eleanor. Sadly, most of those children were either miscarried, stillborn, or died early. As a consequence, only six of them survived.

First, Edward I reigned as the Duke of Aquitaine and

Duke of Gascony from 1249 to 1306. Then, he was the King of England and Lord of Ireland from 1272 to 1307. Finally, he was the Count of Ponthieu with his first wife, Eleanor of Castile, from 1279 to 1290.

Illustrated by Siwon Lee

Here is the picture of King Edward Ⅱ. As you see, he is lying on the bed, unlike other kings. Also, this picture is similar to that of his grandfather King Henry Ⅲ of England.

Edward II

Edward II was born on April 25, 1284. He was the last surviving son of King Edward I and his first wife, Eleanor of Castile. When he was 23, he became the king of England following the death of his father. One year later, Edward married Princess Isabella of France. Isabella was the daughter of King Philippe IV of France and his wife, Queen Joan I of Navarre. They had four children: Edward III; John of Eltham, Earl of Cornwall; Eleanor, Countess of Guelders; and Joan, Queen of Scotland. He also had an illegitimate son named Adam Fitzroy.

During his reign, he did not pay attention to the state affairs. Many years later, there was anarchy in Scotland. Robert the Bruce led a second rebellion against England, and England lost this battle. Then, Robert the Bruce brought Scotland out of anarchy, and Robert declared himself the King of Scotland. He also declared Scotland's independence from England and established Scotland's new dynasty, the House of Bruce.

Edward II wanted to regain authority over Scotland. As we know, Edward's army was defeated by Scotland. While Edward was a lazy king in ruling his country, his wife made a plan to communicate secretly with many French nobles. She wanted her first son Edward to be king instead of her husband. She also wanted to give King Edward's land to Prince Edward. The plan progressed successfully. Then, King Edward II was abdicated from the throne and was imprisoned. Edward II died on September 21, 1327, at the age of 43. He was the king of England for 20 years but never ruled on his own.

First, Edward II was the Count of Ponthieu from 1290 to 1325. Next, he was the Prince of Wales from 1301 to 1307. Then, he was the Duke of Aquitaine from 1306 to 1325. Finally, he was the King of England and Lord of Ireland from 1307 to 1327.

All of those titles except the Prince of Wales were inherited by his son, King Edward III. The Prince of Wales title was succeeded to his grandson, Edward the Black Prince. One interesting fact about Edward II is that his wife had a lover, Roger Mortimer, who was the first Earl of March and the regent of King Edward III until 1330. In addition, Edward II is known as a notorious King of England and is even compared with his great grandfather King John.

다드워드 3세
Edward III)

Illustrated by Siwon Lee

Here is the picture of King Edward III. He is wearing red and blue clothes beneath a blue cape. His clothes represent the traditional design that was used during the 100 Years' War.

Edward III

Edward III was born on November 13, 1312. He was the first son of King Edward II and Isabella of France. His paternal grandparents were Edward I and Eleanor of Castile, and his maternal grandparents were King Philippe IV of France and Queen Joan I of Navarre.

When his father died in 1327, his mother controlled him, making him a weak king. At the age of 17, Edward made the plan that would be successfully completed. His knights seized his controllers. Then, Mortimer, Isabella's lover, was executed, and Isabella was imprisoned.

Scots defeated his forces, and Scotland then made an alliance with France.

In 1328, France's first ruling dynasty, the House of Café, came to an end, and the throne went to Philippe of Valois, but Edward disagreed with this decision. As a result, he decided to go to war with France. This is known as the 100 Years' War (1337-1453). Edward and his son (Edward the Black Prince) won many battles, including the battle that led to the capture of King Jean II. The war was not very easy to win. Unfortunately, Edward's oldest son, Edward the Black Prince, caught dysentery. He lived for ten more years until he died in 1376. In 1377, King Edward died at the age of 64.

The king had 13 children with his wife, Queen Philippa of Hainault: Edward the Black Prince; Isabella, Countess of Bedford; Joan of England; William of Hatfield; Lionel, the first Duke of Clarence; John of Gaunt, the first Duke of Lancaster; Blanche; Edmund, the first Duke of York; Mary of Waltham; Margaret, the Countess of Pembroke; Thomas of Windsor; William of Windsor; and finally Thomas of Woodstock, the first Duke of Gloucester. Only four of his children outlived him: one daughter and three sons. The throne went to his oldest grandson, 10-year-old Richard, who later became Richard II.

Edward III was the Duke of Aquitaine from 1325 to 1360. He was also the Count of Ponthieu from 1325 to 1369, Lord of Aquitaine from 1360 to 1362, and the King of England and Lord of Ireland for 50 years.

Illustrated by Siwon Lee

Here is the picture of King Richard Ⅱ. As you see, he is wearing a cloth that has many accessories. Also, he is sitting on the chair with his sticks. However, he looks sad as a king.

Richard II

Richard II was born on January 6, 1367. He was the second son of Edward the Black Prince and his wife, Joan of Kent. However, when his older brother, Edward, died at the age of five, he became an heir to the English throne. When Richard was nine, his father, Edward the Black Prince, died. One year later, his grandfather Edward III died in 1377, and Richard became King Richard II of England at the age of 10.

As he was not mature enough to run a country, Edward's uncle, John of Gaunt, became his regent. From that point on, John established his own branch: Lancaster. Also, another of the King's uncles, Edmund of York, established another rival branch: York. These two branches became rivals during the Wars of the Roses.

During Richard's reign, England continuously suffered from the bubonic plague, which spread during the Middle Ages. In addition, there was a big rebellion, Wat Tyler's Rebellion, that took place during his reign. Fortunately, Richard successfully suppressed this rebellion.

At the age of 15, Richard was married to Anne of Bohemia, who was the daughter of the Holy Roman Emperor, Charles IV and his last wife, Empress Elizabeth of Pomerania. They were loving spouses, but they did not have any children. Sadly, Queen Anne died of the bubonic plague in 1394 at the age of 28, and Richard mourned her deeply.

Four years later, Richard married Princess Isabella of Valois because he was interested in a peace treaty with France. Isabella was the oldest child of King Charles IV of France and his queen, Isabella of Bavaria. By then, Richard was hated by everyone, and the people wanted the new king. His cousin, Henry, the Duke of Lancaster, led a rebellion that forced Richard to abdicate in 1399. Richard was imprisoned and murdered in 1400 at the age of 33.

First, Richard II was Prince of Wales from 1376 to 1377. Then, he was the Duke of Aquitaine from 1377 to 1390. Finally, he was the King of England and Lord of Ireland from 1377 to 1399.

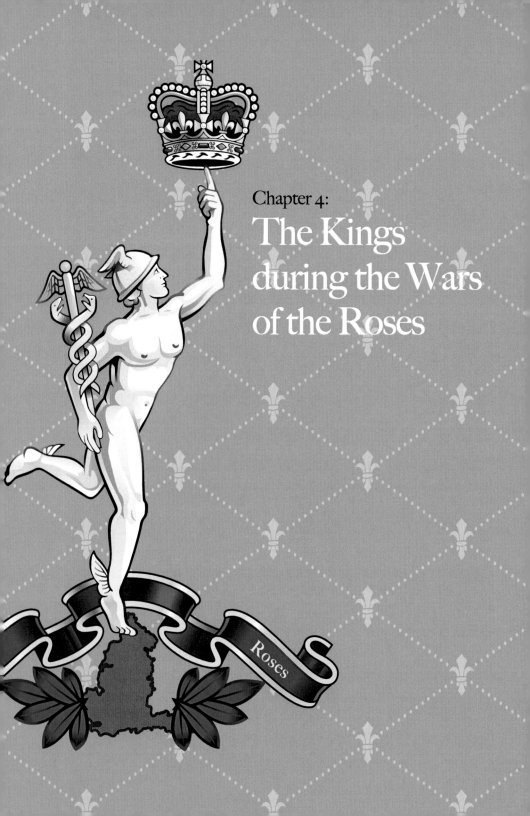

Chapter 4:
The Kings during the Wars of the Roses

John of Gaunt

Edmund of York

John Beaufort

Richard Cambridge

John Beaufort Jr.

Richard of York

Henry IV

Henry V

Edward IV

Richard III

Henry VI

Edward V

Illustrated by Siwon Lee

Here is the picture of King Henry IV. He is wearing a red hat with some jewelry. Also, he is wearing a gold, silver, and red cloth and holding a thin, long gold stick.

Henry IV

Henry IV was born on April 1367. He was the seventh child of John of Gaunt and his first wife, Blanche of Lancaster. He was the grandson of King Edward III. This means he had a right to inherit the English throne. When Henry was one year old, his mother died at the age of 26. Five years later, his father remarried Constance of Castile and had two more children, of which only one survived till adulthood.

In 1380, Henry was married to Mary de Bohun at the age of 13. Six years later, they had their first child, the future King Henry V of England. They had five more children: Thomas of Lancaster, the Duke of Clarence; John of Lancaster, the Duke of Gloucester; Blanche of England; and finally, Philippa of England.

Mary died in 1394 at the age of 23. Five years later, Henry IV's father, John of Gaunt, died at the age of 58. Then, Henry got some French lands, including Aquitaine, and became the Duke of Aquitaine in 1399. However, Richard seized the land and took control of it, except for Aquitaine. As a result, Henry had a reason to attack Richard. In 1399, Henry went to attack Richard and was successful. Henry could now depose Richard from his throne. Henry imprisoned Richard and had him murdered.

In 1403, Henry remarried Joan of Navarre. Joan was first married to John IV, the Duke of Brittany. When John IV died, she was married to Henry. After Henry IV retreated from the power, his son Prince Henry ruled until Henry died on March 20, 1413, at the age of 45.

First, Henry IV was the Earl of Northampton from 1384 to 1399. Then, he was the Duke of Lancaster and Lord High Steward of Scotland in 1399. He was also the Duke of Aquitaine from 1399 to 1400. Finally, he was the King of England and Lord of Ireland from 1399 to 1413.

Here is the picture of King Henry V. As you see, he is not wearing a crown but a brown cape.

Henry V

Henry V was born on September 10, 1386. He was the oldest child of King Henry IV of England and his first wife, Mary de Bohun. When Henry was 12, his father became the King of England by deposing King Richard II. Following this incident, Henry became the Prince of Wales. At the age of 26, Henry became the king of England after his father's death. During his reign, Henry decided to go to war against France.

The French King, Charles VI was a mentally unstable ruler. Henry was able to beat the French easily and invaded most of the French lands. This is why he is known as Henry the Conqueror. So, Henry drew up a treaty with France known as the Treaty of Troyes. There were two promises: First, Henry V would marry Princess Catherine of Valois, the daughter of King Charles VI. Second, Henry V would be King of France after King Charles VI's death. As a result, Henry married Catherine of Valois in 1420 at the age of 33. They had one child, Henry, Prince of Wales.

Henry then went to the battlefield to finish the war. However, he caught dysentery during the battle and died at the age of 35. Fortunately for France, but unfortunately for England, Henry V died before the death of Charles VI. So, the throne went to his eight-month-old son, Henry VI. The wife of Henry V, Catherine Valois, later had many children with her butler, Owen Tudor. Through their son, Catherine became the grandmother of King Henry VII.

Henry V was the Prince of Wales and Duke of Cornwall and Lancaster from 1399 to 1413. He was also the Duke of Aquitaine from 1400 to 1422 and the Lord Warden of Cinque Port from 1409 to 1412. Finally, he was the King of England and Lord of Ireland from 1413 to 1422.

Illustrated by Siwon Lee

Here is a picture of King Henry VI. As you see, he is wearing a black and white cloth, with beautiful gold gems. Also, he is wearing a black hat instead of a crown.

Henry VI

Henry VI was born on December 6, 1422. He was the only son of King Henry V and Queen Catherine of Valois. His paternal grandparents were King Henry IV and Mary de Bohun. Henry's maternal grandparents were King Charles VI of France and Isabella of Bavaria. When he was eight months old, his father, the warrior King Henry V, died of dysentery on the battlefield. His maternal grandfather, King Charles VI of France, died three months later.

Henry VI became the king of England, and according to the treaty Troyes, also became the King of France. However, his uncle Charles, the Dauphin of France, opposed this decision.

Charles wanted his father's crown. As a result, he attacked Orleans with his army. However, as Charles's army was weak, it was defeated at the battle of Orleans. Fortunately, Joan of Arc won many battles against English soldiers, and her French army pushed the English out of their country. The war and battles continued after she died in 1431 at the age of 19.

During this time, Henry could not end the war. He thought as much as he could. However, the lands were lost to the French, and Henry's army was kicked out of France. As Henry was not a spectacular military leader, England lost all lands except for Calais.

Two great achievements were made in King Henry's honor. First, he established two colleges, including the King's College, Cambridge. Second, Henry was married to Margaret of Anjou, the niece of the French King Charles VII. They had one child, Edward of Westminster, Prince of Wales.

Unfortunately, Henry VI was sick and an unstable King of England. The situation led to a civil war. Richard, the Duke of York, tried to occupy the throne while he was Henry's regent. Henry's queen, Margaret of Anjou, personally commanded the battle in Wakefield. Richard of York was killed in this battle, and his head was sent to the Tower of London with a paper crown.

However, York's army won the battle, and Richard's son, the tall and handsome 18-year-old Edward, declared himself the king of England. The rightful king, Henry, was still alive but was exiled to Scotland along with his queen and their son, Edward. In 1471, the Count of Warwick; George Plantagenet, the Duke of Clarence; and the French helped Henry to retake his crown from Edward IV. Edward IV returned from his exile with a stronger army. Henry's son was killed in the battle. Henry himself was captured and imprisoned in the Tower of London. The next day, he was murdered by King Edward.

Henry VI was the Duke of Cornwall and Prince of Wales for nine months. Then, he was the Duke of Aquitaine from 1422 to 1453. Finally, he was the king of England and Lord of Ireland from 1422 to 1461(the first reign) and 1470 to 1471(the second reign).

에드워드4세

Here is one of the famous pictures of King Edward IV. He is wearing beautiful cloth with a gorgeous diamond necklace. Like Henry VI, he is also wearing a black hat.

Edward IV

Edward IV was born on April 28, 1442. He was the third child and second son of Richard of York, the third Duke of York and his wife, Cecily Neville, the Duchess of York. He was the grandson of Edmund of York, the first Duke of York. He was also the great-grandson of Edward III.

When Edward was 12 years of age, his father became the regent of England to King Henry VI. However, his father wanted the throne and so attacked Henry. York's army won the battle, but his father died. This happened in December of 1460. Three months later, Edward became King Edward IV of England at the age of 18. He was a tall and handsome king. Three years later, he was married to a beautiful but poor widow, Elizabeth Woodville. She was the daughter of Richard Woodville, the first Earl Rivers and Jacquetta of Luxembourg.

However, nine years later, one of his supporters, Richard Neville, the 16th Earl of Warwick, betrayed him. Edward's younger brother, George Plantagenet, also betrayed him by marrying Warwick's daughter Isabel, the Duchess of Clarence. The reason why Warwick and George betrayed him was because of Edward's wife. Elizabeth Woodville had first been married to the Lancaster side's supporter, Sir John Grey.

As a result of this, Edward VI and his wife, Elizabeth Woodville, went into exile, and they had their oldest son, Edward. Some months later, Edward returned from his exile with a more powerful army. He murdered Henry VI's son, Prince Edward; and Richard Neville 11th, the 16th Earl of Warwick. In addition to that, Edward also murdered King Henry VI in the Tower of London.

In 1478, King Edward finally murdered his younger brother George Plantagenet by drowning him into the wine. As a result, there was only one Lancasterian left, Henry Tudor of Lancaster. Henry was the son of Edmund Tudor and Margaret Beaufort.

Margaret was the great great granddaughter of King Edward III. In 1483, Edward died of an unknown illness at the age of 40. Before he died, he made his oldest son Edward his heir and his brother Richard as regent.

Edward IV was the Duke of York, Earl of Cambridge, Earl of March, and Earl of Ulster from 1460 to 1461. Then, he was the King of England and Lord of Ireland from 1461 to 1470 and 1471 to 1483.

Even though he was a devoted and faithful husband to his Queen Elizabeth Woodville, one interesting fact about him was his notorious affairs and other illegitimate children. Edward had 10 legitimate children: Elizabeth, Mary, Cecily, Edward, Margaret, Richard, Anne, George, Catherine, and Bridget. He also had three more illegitimate children - Elizabeth, Arthur, and Grace - with his mistresses.

Illustrated by Siwon Lee

   Here is the picture of King Edward V of England. He is wearing a black hat and a red-gold cape. Also, he has a gold stick and a gold circle.

Edward V

Edward V was born on November 2, 1470. He was the oldest son of King Edward IV and Queen Elizabeth Woodville. When he was born, his parents were in exile. One year later, his father retook the crown from Henry VI and eliminated Henry and his supporters. When Edward was 12, his father died of an unknown illness. Edward became King Edward V of England, and his uncle Richard became his regent.

Edward needed to attend his coronation, so his uncle Richard wanted to bring the boy king to London. However, Edward's mother, Elizabeth Woodville, did not trust Richard. Still, Richard brought Edward and his brother, who was also named Richard, to the Tower of London. Richard claimed that this was for their protection. However, the two princes were never seen after that. Richard justified his actions with the rumor that Edward V was an illegitimate son of Edward IV, from before Edward IV married his queen.

Their mother, dowager Queen Elizabeth Woodville fought for her children, but her youngest son was also murdered by Richard. As a result, she decided to form a union with Margaret Beaufort of Lancaster. She also helped Margaret's son Henry to get the throne from her enemy Richard.

In 1674, a workman in the London Tower found two bones. There were some rumors that these were the bones of the two princes. Some years later, the rumors proved to be true. The young princes were perhaps murdered by Richard III or Henry Tudor (Henry VII). Now, Richard became King Richard III of England.

Edward V was the Prince of Wales and the Duke of Cornwall from 1471 to 1483. Then, he was the King of England and Lord of Ireland for two months.

Illustrated by Siwon Lee

Here is the picture of King Richard III of England. As you see, he is wearing a black cloth with fabulous gems. Also, he is wearing a black hat with a gold circle.

Richard III

Richard Ⅲ was born on October 2, 1452. He was the seventh son and 11th child of Richard, the third Duke of York and his wife Cecily Neville. When Richard was eight years old, his father died, and Edward became the King of England in 1461. Richard was made the Lord High Admiral of England in 1462.

However, Richard's brother, George Plantagenet; the Duke of Clarence; and Richard Neville, the 16th Earl of Warwick, betrayed King Edward. Then, they enthroned Henry Ⅵ of Lancaster once again as the King of England. Fortunately, Edward Ⅳ removed Henry Ⅵ from the throne, and Henry's supporters were murdered in 1471. Twelve years later, Edward

IV died at the age of 40.

Now, Richard's nephew, also called Edward became King Edward V, and Richard was appointed as his regent. However, Richard thought that he could be the King of England by eliminating his nephew from the throne. As a result, Richard justified the rumor that Edward V is an illegitimate son of King Edward IV. This meant that Richard was now a rightful heir to the throne of England. He became the King of England in 1483 at the age of 30.

Richard was known as a notorious king of England. In addition to imprisoning the two princes in the Tower of London, it was recorded that he drowned his brother George in the wine and murdered Henry VI's son, Edward, on the battlefield. Then, he married Edward's wealthy widow, Anne Neville.

As a result, many nobles joined Henry of Lancaster to defeat Richard III and take the crown from him. Elizabeth Woodville also supported Henry of Lancaster. In 1484, Richard's only son, Edward of Middleham, died between the age 7 and 11. Richard did not have any heir to inherit the throne. Finally, Richard was killed by Henry Tudor of Lancaster in the battle of Bosworth Field. This battle ended the Wars of the Roses. The same year, his wife Anne Neville died of a disease at the age of 28.

Richard III was first the Lord High Admiral of England from 1462 to 1470 and 1471 to 1483. Then, he was the Lord High Constable of England from 1469 to 1470 and 1471 to 1483. Finally, he was the King of England and Lord Ireland for two years. Richard had two illegitimate children, John and Catherine.

Chapter 5:
The Kings in the House of Tudor

Arthur

Tudor

Here's the picture of King Henry VII. As you see, he is wearing a black hat with valuable gems. He is also wearing a fabulous red cloth with lots of accessories. Unlike other kings, we cannot see his hands.

Henry VII

Henry VII was born on January 28, 1457. He was the only son of Edmund Tudor and his wife, Margaret Beaufort. Henry was the great-great-grandson of John of Gaunt and his second wife, Katherine Swynford. He was also the great-grandson of Charles VI of France and his queen, Isabella of Bavaria. Henry VII's uncle was Henry VI. In addition to that, Henry VII's grandmother, Catherine of Valois, was married to Owen Tudor after her husband, Henry V, died on the battlefield. As a result, King Henry V gave the title of the first Earl of Richmond to his half-brother, Edmund Tudor.

Now, back to history. At the time of King Henry's birth, his father died by the Yorkists in 1456. This means that Henry was a posthumous child. In 1471, Henry VII's uncle, Henry VI and his cousin, Edward of Westminster, were murdered by the Yorkists. Henry VII became the only Lancastrian to get a victory against the Yorkists.

In 1485, Henry Tudor attacked England with his army. Richard III was killed in the battle of the Bosworth fields. England's new ruling dynasty, the House of Tudor, was established through this battle. Henry Tudor became King Henry VII of England.
As Henry wanted to justify his right as the King of England, he married King Edward IV's daughter, Elizabeth of York. They had seven children: Arthur, Prince of Wales; Margaret, Queen of Scotland; Henry VIII, King of England; Elizabeth, Mary, Queen of France; Edmund and Catherine. Sadly, only three of them survived to adulthood.

Henry VII's wife died due to a miscarriage in 1503. Henry VII and his children mourned her deeply, and Henry VII never remarried. He died a widower in 1509 at the age of 52. He was famous for taxing his people heavily.

Henry VII was the Earl of Richmond from 1457 to 1461. Then, he was the King of England and Lord of Ireland from 1485 to

1509. His greatest achievement was ending the Wars of the Roses, bringing in a new era.

Here is the most famous picture of Henry VIII. As you see, it looks like he has mighty power. He is standing in front of a curtain. He has many fabulous gems in his cloth.

Henry VIII

Henry Ⅷ was born on June 28, 1491. He was the third child and the second son of King Henry Ⅶ and his wife, Elizabeth of York. Through his father, he was the descendant of the French king as well as the Lancastrians. He was also a descendant of the Duke of Luxemburg and the Yorkists.

When he was 10, his older brother Arthur, the Prince of Wales, was married to Catherine of Aragon, who was the youngest daughter of Isabel of Castile and Ferdinand Ⅱ of Aragon.

However, Arthur died childless at the age of 15 in 1502, after just one year of marriage. Queen Elizabeth of York also died because of a miscarriage. Henry's father, King Henry Ⅶ, lamented her death and died as a widower in 1509.

Now, Henry became King Henry VIII of England. He was married to his former sister-in-law, Catherine of Aragon, in 1509, when Henry was 17 and Catherine was 23. They had six children: three sons and three daughters. Sadly, Catherine miscarried four times, and one child died early. Therefore, they had only one surviving child, Princess Mary. Henry was very disappointed, and when Catherine reached the age of 40, she became unable to have more children.

As time passed, Henry became more interested in the queen's lady-in-waiting, Anne Boleyn. Her father, Thomas Boleyn, was the first Earl of Wiltshire, the Earl of Ormond, and a diplomat of England. Moreover, Anne's maternal uncle, Thomas Howard, was the third Duke of Norfolk.

As a result, Henry decided to divorce Catherine. At that time, the only person who could handle the royal divorce was the Pope of the Roman Catholic Church. Henry sent a letter to divorce Catherine and marry Anne Boleyn. Catherine, however, sent back a letter to cease the divorce. Fortunately for Catherine, the Pope refused to justify the divorce. Henry's divorce was refused because of the Holy Roman Emperor, Charles V.

The story began when the Pope lost the Italian war. Then, the Pope was under siege by the Holy Roman emperor, Charles V. As Charles was Catherine's nephew, he ordered the Pope to refuse Henry's divorce. Therefore, Henry dissolved England's relationship with Roman Catholic Church and changed the state religion to Protestantism. Then, he declared himself as head of the Church of England. Henry also murdered lots of Catholics and finally divorced Catherine of Aragon.

In 1533, Henry finally married Anne Boleyn. She became the Queen of England when she was between 25 and 32 years of age. They had four children: three sons and one daughter. Unfortunately, Anne miscarried three children and had only one surviving daughter, Princess Elizabeth. Three years later, Anne was beheaded by Henry in the Tower of London.

Only 11 days later, Henry married Anne's lady-in-waiting, Jane Seymour. Jane gave birth to a healthy baby son, Prince Edward. However, Jane died only 12 days later due to an infection after birth. After Jane's death, Henry VIII married three more times. Henry's wives were: Anne of Cleves, whom Henry divorced; Catherine Howard, who was beheaded like Anne Boleyn; and Catherine Parr, who survived after Henry's death in 1547.

However, he had no more legitimate children except Princess Mary, Princess Elizabeth, and Prince Edward. When Henry VIII died on January 28, 1547, at the age of 55, his English throne passed to his youngest son, Prince Edward.

Henry VIII was the Lord Warden of Cinque Port from 1493 to 1509. Then, he was the Earl Marshal from 1494 to 1509, as well as Duke of Cornwall and Prince of Wales from 1502 to 1509. He was also the Lord of Ireland from 1509 to 1542. Finally, he was the King of England from 1509 to 1547. He was the King of Ireland from 1542 to 1547. Henry was the last Lord of Ireland. In 1542, he united the crown of Ireland to the crown of England.

Henry VIII had several illegitimate children with many of his mistresses. One of them was Henry Fitzroy, who was recognized by Henry VIII. He had six more additional children: Thomas Stukeley, Richard Edwardes, Catherine Carey, Henry Carey, Ethelreda Malte, and John Perrot.

Illustrated by Siwon Lee

This is the picture of King Edward VI of England. He is wearing a black cape with black furs. Beneath, he is wearing a fabulous red cloth. He is also wearing a black hat with a small white circle. Finally, he has a book that represents the Protestant Church of England.

Edward VI

Edward VI was born on October 12, 1537. He was the youngest legitimate son of King Henry VIII and his third queen, Jane Seymour. Unfortunately, his mother died soon after his birth, and his father, Henry VIII, died in 1547. Edward became King Edward VI of England at the age of nine.

Edward was a weak king. He caught a disease and was expected to die early. Edward did not have any heir to inherit the throne. This meant that his older sister Mary would inherit the English throne. However, Mary was a Catholic, and Edward was a Protestant. So, Edward opposed Mary as his heir. Instead, he appointed Lady Jane Grey as his successor. As a result, Jane

Gray became the disputed Queen of England when she was beween 15 and 17 years of age after Edward died at the age of 15 in 1553.

Edward VI was the Prince of Wales and the Duke of Cornwall from 1537 to 1547. Then, he was the King of England and King of Ireland from 1547 to 1553.

저은 그레이

Illustrated by Siwon Lee

Here is the picture of the disputed Queen, Lady Jane Grey of England. As you see, she is wearing a red-colored cloth with many beautiful gems. Like Edward VI, she has a book covered in black.

116

Written & illustrated by Siwon Lee.
Designed by macygraph.
Printed in South Korea.